You can do it! Series (Book 1)

Change Your Life for Good

with the PAME Code of Purpose, Action, Momentum, and Energy

Inspired by ground-breaking research and captivating life stories from applied psychology

Dr. E. V. Estacio, Ph.D., C.Psychol., S.F.H.E.A.

Change Your Life for Good by Dr E V Estacio
Published by the PAME Code Publishing

www.thepamecode.com

For permissions contact: info@thepamecode.com

Editor: Nicole Langston

Cover concept by 100 Covers
Final cover edited by Edelitz Estacio

ISBN-13: 978-1981763986
ISBN-10: 1981763988

I also acknowledge the helpful comments of my test readers to an earlier version of this book. Special thanks to Catherine Sykes, Dennis Cortez, and Sue Plumtree for inspiring me to take this step, to Gundi Gabrielle and all my folks at SassyZenGirl for demystifying the publication process for me, and to all my friends and family for all the encouragement and support.

Disclaimer

This book is designed to provide information and motivation to our readers. While all attempts have been made to verify the information provided in this publication, neither the Author, nor the Publisher assumes any responsibility for errors, omissions, or contrary interpretations on the subject matter herein.

Any perceived slight of any individual or organization is purely unintentional.

The book is sold with the understanding that neither the Author, nor the Publisher is engaged to render any type of psychological, medical, legal, or any other kind of professional advice. Neither the Author nor the Publisher shall be held liable or responsible to any person or entity with respect to any physical, psychological, emotional, financial, or commercial damages, including, but not limited to, special, incidental, consequential or other damages, or alleged to have been caused, directly or indirectly, by the information or programs contained herein. Every person is different and the advice and strategies contained herein may not be suitable for your situation.

Our views and rights are the same:

You are responsible for your own choices, actions, and results.

CONTENTS

FREE BONUS

Congratulations!

You have taken a step to changing your life for good.

To help you in this journey, I have compiled **60 motivational quotes** from remarkable individuals from all over the world.

May you find encouragement from these tiny pearls of wisdom and live the life you truly deserve.

Download your free bonus at **www.thepamecode.com/bonus**

DEDICATION

To my parents for life.

To my Andy for love.

To my friends for encouragement.

And to my Vas for my purpose – thank you!

PREFACE

Change your life for good – that's a big one!

Change is not always easy.

It takes *massive courage* to admit that change is needed – and a whole lot more to act and make it happen.

When it comes to dramatic changes in life, you need to have the right tools and support to help you get the results you desire.

In this book, we will unlock what I would call, *"the PAME Code"*, so you can begin to drive the change you need in your life.

What is the PAME Code?

Coming from someone who married a Greek man, PAME has become a permanent fixture in my vocabulary.

It is pronounced "pāhmeh" and it means, *"let's go together"*.

Or when it comes from my husband, it means, *"c'mon, let's go NOW!"*

Obviously, I hear this when he wants me to pick up my feet and get moving.

In the same way, I will borrow these words so you too can pick up your feet and get going.

In this book, PAME stands for:

P	Purpose
A	Action
M	Momentum
E	Energy

PAME will be a reminder that we need to have a clear *purpose*, first and foremost. We need to follow this up with real *action*, maintain our *momentum*, and keep up the *energy* to sustain progress.

A fair warning: it is not always going to be a smooth ride – just learn from my experience.

My story

I am an academic - a psychologist who specializes in community development and health promotion to be specific.

Ever since I was a little girl, I have always been driven by academic achievement. I was the one with the nerdy glasses, chunky braces, baggy clothes, and neon socks.

I was *obsessed* with getting top marks in class, so I could get into the best universities, become an accomplished academic, and gain international credibility in my profession.

To some extent, I achieved these goals at a relatively young age.

At age 15, I was accepted into an accelerated University program to study medicine. However, following the generous advice of my mother, I studied psychology as a pre-med course instead. I completed my degree with flying colors and graduated magna cum laude four years later.

I enjoyed studying psychology so much that I decided to pursue a post-graduate education.

I moved to London and gained my Ph.D. by the time I was 24.

I took up competitive academic positions, became an international best-selling author, sat on several scientific editorial boards, and achieved an international reputation in my field of expertise.

Of course, I achieved all of this with *tremendous* and *unwavering* support from immediate family, friends, and the then-strangers who are now my closest and best mentors and allies.

Alongside this (although this was not part of *my* original plan), family life was also going splendidly well. I met someone incredible. Got married. Had a baby.

Life was sweet.

Then, depression and anxiety hit me.

Following a challenging return to work after maternity leave, my world was turned upside down.

I will not go into detail about this experience here, but I can say that it was agonizingly painful, if not traumatic.

It almost cost me my life.

It may have been a difficult experience, but looking back now, I can say with certainty that it was necessary.

It hurt. Deeply.

But in the end, this dark period in my life turned out to be a blessing.

Because of this experience, I re-oriented my gaze and re-prioritized my life. I am now putting my efforts into what truly matters to me rather than wasting my time on things that don't.

I also gained more empathy and compassion for those who are still in the dark and for those who are struggling to find their way out.

With my family by my side, I found a renewed passion and a real sense of purpose in life. I can now see my life and the direction I want to take more clearly than ever before.

Life was sweet.

But now that I have tasted *bitter*, life now tastes even *better*.

I appreciate it all the more.

The techniques described in this book are some of the strategies I have used to find my purpose and the steps I am (still) taking to fulfill it.

Of course, being a psychologist, I could not help but look for the best evidence-based practice to help all of us.

Yes, that's right – us – that means you, me and anyone else who might need help.

My story is not finished. Neither is yours.

My hope is for this book to be useful for all of us.

May the ideas and strategies outlined in this book help you live the purposeful life you're meant to live as much as they are helping me to live mine. <3

How to make the most of this book

1. **Start from the beginning** and read in a chronological order. The book will make more sense this way.
2. **Be aware of your inner critics** and replace them with more helpful thoughts using the techniques discussed in this book, especially if they are interfering with your progress.

"Inner critic? What's that?" you ask.

The inner critic is a tiny voice that lives inside your head.

Sometimes it tells you helpful things. Sometimes it does not. Sometimes you will hear it say, "You'll never be good enough." And sometimes you will hear it say, "Just give up!"

We all have an inner critic living inside our head.

However, unlike other self-help books that will ask you to silence, crush, or even banish your inner critic, this book will ask you to listen to it.

Be aware and listen to your inner critic.

- What is it saying?
- Where are these views coming from?
- Why is it saying that particular thing?

The reason why you need to listen to your critic rather than quiet it down is because this inner critic, whether you like it or not, is still part of who you are.

By silencing, crushing, or banishing it, you are putting yourself at risk of having a battle with yourself; a battle you have little hope of winning.

Instead, you need to listen, understand, but not necessarily follow.

Try to see where this critic is coming from and aim to convince it to come to your side using alternative and more positive messages.

Convince and reconcile.

This way, you can eventually both play on the same team, move toward the same direction, and manifest the life you truly deserve.

3. **Take notes**, with pen and paper, if you can. Research suggests that writing your notes by hand will help you to understand and remember the material better. Write down your ideas and reflect on these as you go along. If writing by hand does not suit you, the next best thing is to record your notes using whatever platform works for you.
4. **Have a go** at some of the strategies suggested in this book. See if they work for you. If you find yourself struggling, try to tailor the strategies to suit your personality and circumstances.
5. **Find a buddy** to talk to as you go through the strategies outlined in this book. It could be your pastor or religious leader, a friend, your partner, your therapist or coach. Find someone you trust to share your thoughts and progress as you go through this book.

You will find prompts throughout this book that will ask you to actively engage with the points mentioned above. To help you spot these action prompts easily, I have added the following icons throughout the text:

As the first of the YOU CAN DO IT! Series, this book will help you take the baby steps you need so you can radically transform your life, unleash the real you, and live your true purpose in life.

Are you ready to Change your Life for Good, the PAME way?

Then, PAME! (let's go together!)

CHAPTER 1

PURPOSE

There are many definitions of purpose.

The simplest one I have found so far referred to purpose as *"the reason for which something is done or created or for which something exists."*

Why are we here? Why do we exist? What are we doing with our lives?

What is our purpose in life?

If you are looking for the *ultimate* answer to these questions, then this is probably not the book for you.

This book will NOT answer these questions for you.

Instead, this book will help you to take small steps to gradually unravel your life's purpose – and get on with it.

Your life's purpose is a work in progress.

It is important that you recognize what it is and take the necessary steps to fulfill it before you run out of time.

Why finding your purpose is important

It is simple. Finding your purpose will help you focus.

By aligning your purpose with your actions, your time will be better spent doing things that are meaningful to you.

Scientific research also suggests that having a sense of life calling or purpose is associated with success.

Why?

Because people who are living a life of purpose become driven.

They become unstoppable because they know that there is a reason, sometimes higher than themselves, for their existence.

Decades of psychological research illustrate that having a purpose in life is associated with having a sense of harmony and peace, and is linked with better health and well-being.

A life lived based on purpose is also more fulfilling and fun.

Life simply becomes more enjoyable when you are aiming to fulfill your purpose.

Start with the *what* and the *why* in your life – and everything else will follow.

INNER CRITIC ALERT
I know that having a purpose in life is important. But I have NO clue what mine is and how to find it. It's all very complicated.

Do not fret. You are not the only one who hears this from their inner critic.

Help is on the way!

START uncovering your life's purpose
using the PASTLE technique

There are many ways to uncover your purpose.

Our libraries are filled with books that go into *too much* detail on how to do this. I won't do that here.

Instead, I will keep it *very* simple so you can use this strategy as soon as possible.

I do not claim that this is the only strategy you must follow. There are many ways to uncover your purpose.

By all means, follow the process that suits you.

However, the process I will share here is the one that has worked for me and for others I know.

Hopefully, you will find it useful too.

Are you ready to *start* uncovering your life's purpose?

PAME! (let's go together!)

GO	**HAVE A GO!**

The PASTLE technique: PAssion + STrength + LEgacy = Purpose

INSTRUCTIONS

This exercise is called the PASTLE technique. You are asked to follow the 4 steps below and answer the questions as honestly as possible. You can either write down your answers OR you can ask your buddy to go through the questions with you while they write down your responses.

Take your time to reflect, but please, do NOT overthink.

ANSWER WITH YOUR GUT.

STEP 1: KNOW WHAT IS IMPORTANT TO YOU (YOUR PASSION)

a. <u>Identify what is important to you</u>

What do you consider important in your life? (e.g., relationships; career; social justice; abundance; nature; art; sexuality; health; spirituality; well-being, etc.).

List everything you consider important. Don't filter anything. Just write it all down.

If you are stuck and need a bit of help getting started, these 23 powerful prompt questions can really help.
Visit: http://sassyzengirl.com/find-your-passion-purpose/

b. Rate your CURRENT status ("where you are right now")

Once you have identified aspects of your life that you consider important, I want you to explore how you feel about these aspects currently in your life.

Think about how satisfied you are with your interaction and involvement with that specific aspect in your life.

"Can you be doing more?"
"Can you devote more time, effort, or resources to this?"
"Can you give it the attention it deserves?"

On a scale of 0-10, how satisfied are you with these RIGHT NOW (0=not at all satisfied; 10=completely satisfied)

For example, I would say that *my family* is important to me. Right now, on a scale of 0-10, I would say I am currently at 7. My family is great, but I would like to spend more quality time with them.

Likewise, I would say that *a compassionate society* is very important to me. On a scale of 0-10, I am currently at 4, because I know I can do more to contribute to this.

c. Rate your DESIRED status ("where you want to be")

On a scale of 0-10, how satisfied would you WANT TO BE with these aspects in your life (0=not at all satisfied; 10=completely satisfied).

In my case, I want to raise *my family* satisfaction from 7 to 10. This is a priority since time spent to build *childhood memories* with my growing son is limited.

Likewise, I would like to raise my ability to contribute to building a more *compassionate society* from 4, to at least 8, at the time being. I want my son and future generations to grow up in an environment that values compassion and respect for others.

d. Rank and prioritize

Based on your answers above, rank and prioritize what you value in life. This will uncover your *passions in life*.

It is entirely up to you how you would do this.

According to Humanist Psychologist, Carl Rogers, we all have the basic human motive to fulfill our potential. He referred to this as *"self-actualization"*.

It is about being able to express the deepest and most sincere version of ourselves. This process is achieved when our ideal and real selves are congruent with each other.

Narrowing the gap between *"where you are right now"* and *"where you want to be"* can help to minimize the gap between your real and ideal selves.

 TALK TO YOUR BUDDY

You can ask your buddy to help you rank and prioritize your passions. For this exercise, you will need:

- Notecards – so you can write on separate cards what you feel is important to you
- Pen and paper (or a recorder) – so your buddy can record your responses and thought processes.

You can use the notecards to rank and prioritize your passions in life. Get your buddy involved by having them ask you to elaborate and reflect more deeply on why you consider some aspects more important than others.

Not only is this exercise fun and engaging – it will also stimulate critical reflection and help you to uncover deeply-rooted values that you hold dear.

This exercise also has the potential to build a closer relationship between you and your buddy. It's healthy to have a close friend we can trust and share deep things with.

STEP 2: KNOW YOUR TALENTS (YOUR STRENGTH)

Research has shown that people who have the opportunity to act upon their strengths are far more likely to flourish.

It is important that you are able to identify what you are good at and to make the most of your talents.

☒	**INNER CRITIC ALERT**

I am not good at anything.
I have no talents. I have no strengths.
I only have flaws.
I am afraid my weaknesses will be exposed.

If you are like me, someone who has one of these silly voices, my advice is to engage in a dialogue and convince this voice that you also have something *special* that you can share with others.

Everyone has a talent. Tell your inner critics what yours are.

Not sure what your talents are?

Let me help you with that:

- Think about something that you love doing – something that makes you feel alive every time you do it!
- Now, think about something you can do well, it comes naturally and it is easy (and enjoyable!) for you. Relish that thought.
- Next, think about a time someone complimented you on something you did. Or about a time someone said something nice about your personal characteristics or traits.
- Now, think about your greatest accomplishment.

  What is it?

  What personal traits or skills were at the forefront when you achieved these praise worthy deeds?

  Got it? Great!

See, you have talents.

You just need to dig deep, recognize what you have and be grateful for it.

> If you are still stuck and can't figure out your strengths, you could visit, https://tinyurl.com/pamesurvey to get some inspiration.

This questionnaire is developed by Professor Chris Peterson from Michigan University and is designed to highlight your greatest character strengths, ones that you may not even be aware of.

	INNER CRITIC ALERT
	Sure, sure. I have talents. But I am not perfect. I have limitations too.

Of course you do. That's what makes you human!

We are all a work in progress.

> If you are already perfect, then there wouldn't be any more room for growth.

We all have limitations – that's for sure.

But overcoming limitations is also a strength.

> Overcoming adversity requires strength.

> Think about a time when you faced a struggle and overcame it.

> > What characteristics did you possess to help you face your difficulties?

> > Where did you draw your strengths from?

> > Can you draw upon these strengths again when difficulties arise in the future?

Turn your limitations into opportunities for growth.

> Some strengths you were born with.

> Others, you develop along the way.

Your strengths accumulate and you carry these with you as you move forward with your life.

STEP 3: DECLARE WHAT YOU WANT TO CONTRIBUTE (YOUR LEGACY)

Traditionally, most people think of a legacy in terms of money or property left to someone in a will.

But legacy is so much more than that.

Legacy, as we will refer to it in this context, is a part of you that you will leave behind at the end of your life.

How will you be remembered?

How have you touched other people's lives?

What problems would you have solved (or created) in your life?

What circumstances exist now because of the things you have done?

Although legacy is commonly associated with end-of-life, there are no rules regarding when you can start reflecting upon and working towards your legacy.

> **The sooner you think about your legacy, the sooner you can work towards the life you want to be remembered for.**

Research suggests that reflecting upon your legacy can help you to clarify your values and beliefs.

Having your legacy documented in a more tangible manner can also help you to crystallize your purpose in life.

Write your autobituary or your ethical will

An obituary is a notice of death, usually in a newspaper, which typically includes a brief account of the person's life and legacy.

If you had to write your own obituary, or in this case, your *autobituary*, what would it look like?

- What would your obituary say?
- What kind of person will it reflect?
- What were you passionate about and how did these passions manifest in your life?
- What meaningful contributions did you leave behind?

If writing your autobituary is a bit too morbid, you may also consider writing your ethical will.

Unlike a legal will, which conveys your will concerning inheritance of properties and other assets, an *ethical will* is designed to pass on your memories, values, beliefs, life lessons, and wishes to the next generation.

- What will your ethical will contain?
- What would your life story sound like and what lessons will the next generation learn from your story?
- What messages will you leave behind and what values will your life embody?

STEP 4: WRITE YOUR STATEMENT OF PURPOSE

After thinking about your passion, strengths, and legacy (PASTLE), it is now time to write down your purpose.

There may be multiple facets for your purpose (e.g., your relationships, hobby, work, etc.), but there should be a common, underlying purpose for whatever you do.

Go through your PASTLEs and get a sense of what this purpose is.

Scribble down a few things.

It does not matter if it is a thoughtfully written draft or a less organized stream of thought.

The important thing is that you write it all down.

INNER CRITIC ALERT

All of this stuff about writing about my thoughts is stupid!
None of this is going to matter in the end.
There is no point in writing it down.

Writing it down is optional, of course. But so is success.

If you are serious about fulfilling your life's purpose, you will have a better chance of achieving it if you stay focused.

Having a constant reminder of what you set out to do in the first place will help you maintain this focus.

As the saying goes, *"When you're up to your neck in alligators, it's easy to forget you came to drain the swamp."*

You are bound to face obstacles when you aim for your dreams and aspirations.

It is very easy to get distracted by trivial tasks and worries.

Writing down your purpose will remind you of what you set out to do in the first place.

Writing is a highly-structured and systematic process that requires you to organize and make sense of your thoughts.

Research has shown that writing will help you put your thoughts together in a more coherent manner.

It can be very difficult to let your thoughts simply float in your head.

Keeping thoughts up in the air can also feel overwhelming sometimes. Writing them down, in a sense, helps release them.

Plus, there is also the risk of these thoughts evaporating into thin air when the going gets tough.

So, <u>write it down</u>.

> What is important to you? (PAssion)
>
> What are you good at? (STrength)
>
> What do you want to contribute in this lifetime? (LEgacy)

Outline your PAssion, STrength, and LEgacy, to uncover your PURPOSE.

 WRITE YOUR STATEMENT OF PURPOSE

Write your statement of purpose

> Write a few words to state your purpose in life.
> Sleep on it.
> Review it the next day.
> Discuss it with someone (if you like).

Keep writing and refining your statement of purpose until you are comfortable with it.

When you are reasonably happy with what you have written, post it where you'll see it every day.

> Laminate it if you must.
> In this digital age, you can also keep it on the platform you use the most (e.g., your desktop, smartphone, tablet).

However you choose to approach your statement of purpose, the important thing is that you actually do <u>write it down.</u>

I cannot stress the importance of writing it down enough!

As an example, here is my personal statement of purpose:

"To help others to embody their passions and core values so they can meaningfully and fruitfully live their lives to the fullest."

Now that you have written down your purpose, the next thing to do is to envision your FUTURE PERFECT.

What does this mean?

It means creating a mental (or it could be an actual) picture of what your ideal future would look like.

Creating a vivid picture of your hopes and aspirations can really keep you focused on what you are striving for.

Whether it is something for yourself, your family, your organization, your community, or society at large, trying to imagine this *future perfect* will encourage you to open up to the possibility of turning it into reality.

> **You can build whatever you want with your imagination.**
>
> **The only limit is what YOU set it to be.**

This is a really *enjoyable* process which can get your creative juices going!

Be free.

Explore.

The possibilities are endless.

The power of visualization

Visualization can be a very effective way to stimulate your imagination and encourage your mind and body to become accustomed to this imagined ideal scenario. Just look at the research evidence:

Visualization has been shown to improve muscular strength among patients going through physical rehabilitation, such as people recovering from a stroke or spinal cord injury, or those with Parkinson's disease.

Visualization has helped people with social anxiety by encouraging them to imagine being in control in contexts that would normally cause them fear or panic.

Neuroscientific research has also shown that a person who visualizes acting out particular tasks activate the same brain and neural activities as carrying out these tasks.

No wonder decades of scientific research have accumulated vast evidence on how visualization can effectively help athletes, musicians, dancers, public speakers, astronauts, and surgeons to perform their ultimate best, despite the pressures they are exposed to.

By *"rehearsing"* and visualizing these scenarios in their mind it helps them to *"feel and experience"* their perfect performance, even before it happens.

In the same way, visualizing your *future perfect* could be seen as rehearsing your ideal future scenario in your mind before it manifests into reality.

Be optimistic.

INNER CRITIC ALERT
I can't be optimistic. There's nothing to be optimistic about. Besides, being optimistic is like burying your head in the sand. It's a recipe for self-deception.

I am sorry, but you have to tell your inner critic that it is sooooo wrong!

According to scientific research, optimists are actually more vigilant of risks and threats than pessimists.

This means that while some people may be aware of problems but do nothing about them, optimists are very much aware that positive outcomes are dependent on their willingness to do something.

Optimists are aware that they are responsible for their actions; and that these actions have consequences. They look forward to positive outcomes and they do something to make these happen.

Life doesn't happen to them. Life happens because of them.

Envisioning your best possible future can also significantly boost your positive mental attitude, increase feelings of being connected with others, and improve your general health and well-being.

> An experiment by Professor Laura King from the University of Missouri-Columbia has shown that people who wrote about their life's purpose for 20 minutes a day over several days were more likely to show immediate increases in positive moods, were happier several weeks later, and reported fewer physical ailments months after, compared to those who wrote about other topics.

Research has also shown that optimists are also more likely to persevere and overcome difficulties.

> If you have something to look forward to, you will feel energized, motivated and enthusiastic about life.

> You will feel good about yourself.

> You will feel more in control of your destiny (or if you are religious, you will feel you are in safe hands because God is in control).

Optimism will make you unstoppable.

So, are you ready to visualize your future perfect?

PAME! (let's go together!)

 HAVE A GO!

Visualize your FUTURE PERFECT

Imagine your future perfect through relaxation and visualization. **Please do this exercise only when it is safe to do so.** Allocate between 10-15 distraction-free minutes for this.

If you prefer guided relaxation and meditation, I prepared a YouTube video that you can play in the background to help you with this process.

Visit: https://tinyurl.com/pamefuture

Step 1: Find a comfortable position in a quiet environment.

Step 2: When in a comfortable position, begin the exercise by concentrating on your breathing. Breathe in deeply and breathe out slowly. Relax. Feel the rhythm of your breath. You may close your eyes if this helps. As you inhale deeply, you breathe in relaxation. As you exhale slowly, you breathe out tension. Repeat this process until you feel fully relaxed.

Step 3: When you are ready, imagine this scenario:

> *You are in a place and time where you have lived your perfect life. You became who you wanted to become and did what you wanted to do with your life.*

> *Imagine you are in your most favorite spot in the world. Imagine this as vividly as you can. Hear the sounds. See the sights. You smell familiar and relaxing scents.*

> *You feel comfortable and secure in this environment.*

> *In this safe space, imagine yourself spending time reminiscing about the full life you have lived. You see yourself writing your story.*

> *You remember the people you have met along the way. You smile as you remember the times you spent with them. You remember the relationships and adventures you experienced with them.*

> *You remember the places you've been to and the places you called home. You lived a full life.*

> *You also remember how your talents and strengths have been used to the fullest. You remember how you flourished with what you did. You feel satisfied and enriched for being able to express what you truly felt passionate about.*

> *You feel grateful for your life. You lived a full life.*

> *You start writing about your legacy.*

> *You feel a gush of positive emotions as you remember how your efforts have enriched the lives of others.*

> *Be aware of these positive emotions.*

> *Dwell on these feelings. Cherish these feelings.*

Step 4: When you feel ready, slowly return your consciousness to your outside environment, feeling positively energized by imagining your future perfect.

***

This exercise is only an example of how to imagine your future perfect.

If you are able, I strongly encourage you to find a way to embed this practice in your daily routine if you can.

> Some people do this as soon as they wake up in the morning.

> Others do it just before they go to sleep at night. Just find a quiet space and time to relax and meditate.

> However, if you can't find 10-15 minutes of quiet time every day, just try to find time within your routine where you can reflect and imagine your future perfect.

>> Perhaps, you can daydream while putting on your makeup; or perhaps while you are relaxing at home on your sofa.

>> I personally reflect on my future perfect when I have my quiet time in the shower.

>> Since I had my little one, shower time is really the only "me-time" I have. I imagine my future perfect as I cleanse my body from the tension and dirt of the day.

>> Really refreshing I must say!

***

Apart from relaxation and visualization, if you are like me and would prefer something more tangible, then perhaps you can have a go at creating an *actual* visual image of your future perfect.

Create an actual VISUAL IMAGE of your FUTURE PERFECT

This means creating an actual picture or drawing of your future perfect.

Don't worry if you are not an artist. It doesn't have to look pretty.

It just needs to make sense to YOU to help you visualize what you are striving for.

Step 1: Go through your PASTLE notes.

Step 2: Pick out relevant keywords you want to include in your image of your future perfect.

Step 3: Put together images that represent these keywords.

If you are able, draw these images yourself.

However, if like me, you have no artistic talent whatsoever, you can use images from magazines and literally cut and paste these together.

OR

You can search for images online and compile these to create a collage. The SnapCollage app is a really useful tool to do this. There are also good reviews for PicCollage.

When compiling visual images of your future perfect, be sure to **include images of how others are also flourishing** from this ideal scenario.

It could be an image of your family having a healthy and happy life, or perhaps an image of your community achieving common goals and aspirations.

Have fun with this process.

This can be a really enjoyable experience and an opportunity for you to get creative.

Step 4: When you have crafted your visual image, you may want to add your statement of purpose in the image too.

Step 5: Place this image somewhere you can see it every day.

You can frame it if you like, and place it on your work desk.

***

During my childhood, I posted images and words of inspiration in my closet, so that I would see them every time I changed my clothes.

As a grown-up, I have my statement of purpose and visual image of my future perfect saved on my tablet. I reflect on these before I look at my appointments or check my emails.

Embedding this into my daily routine helps me to get into the right mindset and remind myself of what I ultimately want with my life.

Embodying your purpose in life

Now that you have a general understanding of your purpose and what your future perfect could look like, you will need to embed these into your daily routine so that they will essentially become your destiny.

To quote Mahatma Gandhi,

"Your beliefs become your thoughts,
Your thoughts become your words,
Your words become your actions,
Your actions become your habits,
Your habits become your values,
Your values become your destiny."

Try, as much as you can, to live and EMBODY YOUR PURPOSE.

I mean, literally.

Embody your purpose and use your body parts to remind yourself, in every moment of every day, what your life is for.

Let your head be a reminder of your thoughts; your lips of your words; your heart of your emotions; your hands of your actions; and your legs and feet for the steps that you make.

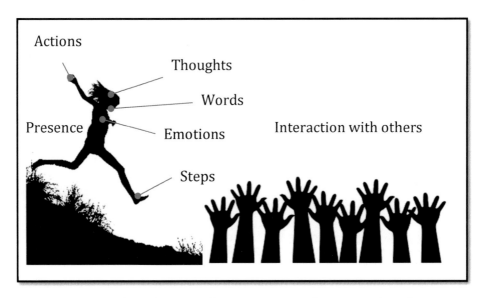

Be mindful of your thoughts, words, emotions, and actions. Are these congruent with your values and what you declared are important to you?

Be aware of the steps you take. Will these make good use of your strengths and talents?

Be mindful of your presence and your interactions with others. Are you projecting yourself the way you want to be remembered?

Always remember the purpose you've set out to accomplish.

Make a pledge to fulfill this purpose and be mindful of how you embody your destiny **from this point forward.**

CHAPTER 2

ACTION

This chapter is called ACTION because this is exactly what it will ask of you.

Unlike other self-help books that have you come up with SMART goals to plan action, this chapter will simply ask you to START acting upon your goals.

DOING rather than just PLANNING – that's what it's all about.

ACTION means ACTION.

Why SMART goals won't work here

Goal setting is the bread and butter of many organizational, health, education, and community psychologists.

Setting SMART goals is a particularly popular goal-setting strategy.

> Whether it is to help businesses achieve sales targets, enhance students' exam performance, or support individuals to change "unhealthy" behavior, SMART goals are widely used to develop action plans to achieve desired results.

There are many versions of what SMART goals mean.

However, in its simplest form, it refers to goals that are:

S	Specific
M	Measurable
A	Action-oriented
R	Realistic
T	Time-bound

SMART goals may be useful in setting short-term goals that have tried and tested routes to success.

However, fulfilling one's purpose in life is far more complex.

SMART goals may not be suitable in this context.

Why?

Two reasons:

1. SMART goals rely only on what you currently know.
2. We are hard-wired to avoid change.

SMART GOALS RELY ONLY ON WHAT WE KNOW

Preparing SMART goals to plan your life's purpose is NOT smart because it only relies on what you currently know.

As you begin to take action to fulfill your purpose, you will realize there are many things you don't know.

You will also discover there are many things that you didn't know you knew, and things that you didn't know you didn't know.

Confusing, huh?

Let me show you the KNOWLEDGE-AWARENESS QUADRANT to explain it better.

KNOWLEDGE-AWARENESS QUADRANT

		AWARENESS	
		Aware	Unaware
KNOWLEDGE	Known	TIP OF THE ICEBERG	HIDDEN TREASURE
	Unknown	IDKs	THE ABYSS

The KNOWLEDGE-AWARENESS QUADRANT consists of four cells that determine what you know and what you are aware of:

1. *Tip of the iceberg*

   You are *aware* that you *know* these things.

   Being aware that you know certain things can help you plan and organize what you need to do.

   However, since this is only the *tip of the iceberg,* there are more things underneath that you need to explore.

2. *IDKs (I don't knows)*

   You are *aware* that you *don't know* these things.

   This is about recognizing your limitations and knowing that there are things that you still don't know.

   Being aware of your IDKs enables you to find room for growth and to recognize that you might need some help in these areas.

   It also allows you to be cautious of your imperfections and work on them.

3. *Hidden treasure*

   You are *not aware* that you *know* these things.

   This is your hidden knowledge, talents, and skills that you are not even aware you possess.

   Hidden treasures are usually uncovered in unexpected circumstances (e.g., in difficult situations where you need to try different approaches to solve a crisis).

   It is important to embrace these hidden treasures when uncovered and to cultivate them to maximize your potential.

4. *The abyss*

   You are *not aware* that you *don't know* these things.

   This is what Donald Rumsfeld would call "the unknown unknowns."

   The abyss will come into light as you gain more awareness through experience.

Shedding light into the abyss can be enlightening, frightening and shocking, all at the same time.

Things in the abyss usually come to the surface when you least expect it.

Let me share with you how this KNOWLEDGE-AWARENESS quadrant can be used in real life.

Here's an example from my experience:

		AWARENESS	
		Aware	Unaware
KNOWLEDGE	Known	TIP OF THE ICEBERG I am aware that I am blessed with skills that I can use to benefit others (e.g., teaching, mentoring, action research)	HIDDEN TREASURE I was not aware that I know how to love unconditionally (until my son was born)
	Unknown	IDKs I am aware that there are still a lot of things that I need to know (e.g., I love cake but I still don't know how to bake one)	THE ABYSS I was not aware that the industry I am in is just a microcosm of society (until I experienced, first-hand, the good, the bad, and the ugly faces of academic life)

Setting SMART goals at this stage will be limited because you are only basing your plan on the tip of your iceberg.

What you need is *real action* so you can gain *real experience*.

Experience widens your awareness.

When you widen your awareness, the *tip of your iceberg* will grow and some of your *hidden treasures* may be uncovered.

At the same time, your *IDKs* may also grow and some light may also be shed into your *abyss*.

> Because the irony is, the more you know, the more you realize that you DON'T know a lot more.

This might scare some people off and those who are faint at heart might give up at this stage.

> But you will need to find a way to turn your IDKs into IFOs (I'll find outs) and to embrace your widened awareness to further enlighten your abyss.

Keep doing (and learning) from experience rather than just planning.

> This is how you will grow.

WE ARE HARD-WIRED TO AVOID CHANGE

The second reason why setting SMART goals can be problematic in this context has to do with how our brain operates.

> You see, our brain works in a rather protective way that tries to maintain a comfortable, balanced state and avoids discomfort caused by change.

> > When you try to develop SMART goals, you flood your brain with thoughts about change.

The problem is, when you feed your brain with thoughts of substantial changes in your *behavior* (e.g., I will exercise more) or your *circumstances* (e.g., I will quit my job), it will also send you messages that tell you that it's scary and that you shouldn't do it.

> Why?

Because the brain will try to protect you from the risk of disturbing the comfortable, stable state that you are in right now.

> *"It's familiar, it's safe. Why do something else?"*

Thoughts of change will also send signals of the risk of failure.

This is the brain's mechanism to protect you from harm.

Because with change, also comes the risk of harm.

This harm can be:

physical (e.g., I might injure myself),

financial (e.g., I might lose my income),

social (e.g., I might lose my friends), or

psychological (e.g., I might lose my mind).

This will trigger a major crisis between you and your inner critic!

Your inner critic will hit you very hard when you are planning SMART goals for the long-term because this process will make you OVER THINK.

If you do not have the strategies to overcome these messages, chances are you will follow your inner critic's voice and avoid change.

Your brain will tell you to do so because we are hard-wired to protect ourselves from perceived harm, real or otherwise.

This is why it is important to have strategies in place to recondition your brain to embrace the change you desire.

How to recondition your brain to embrace change

One strategy is a visualization of your future perfect (remember Chapter 1).

Visualization helps you to become more familiar and comfortable with the future you desire.

While in a relaxed state, visualization can help to minimize the fear and discomfort triggered by thoughts of potential change by encouraging your brain to embrace this reality as something pleasurable, comfortable and desired.

Visualization helps you to "practice" the change before you physically do it – almost like a test run to get used to it.

It's a fear of the unknown that drives us away from change.

"Experiencing" it beforehand through visualization can help elevate some of the unknown.

Another strategy is simply taking small, achievable baby steps to get the ball rolling.

This is a way to desensitize your brain to change.

Take a step and tell your brain that these changes are pleasurable, comfortable and desired.

To reiterate the point of this chapter: take ACTION and get on with it.

Are you ready to take steps toward real action?

PAME! (let's go together!)

 HAVE A GO!

Taking REAL steps toward REAL action

STEP 1: GET A MAP

When you are heading somewhere you've never been before, it's beneficial to bring a map with you.

OK, you don't need to take this literally (but you can if you want to, especially if you're very visual like me).

When you have your map, you need to identify your starting point, your destination, and your Stop A.

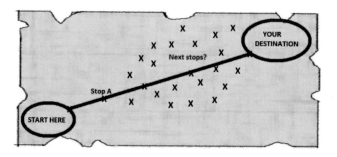

Like with any navigation system, before setting off, you MUST first identify your: 1) <u>starting point</u> and 2) <u>destination</u>.

Your *starting point* is where you are now.

Your *destination* is your stated purpose in life.

> If you had a go at the strategies discussed in Chapter 1, you would have a written draft, or at least some scribbly notes, of your purpose by now.
>
> If you are still clueless and don't know WHAT and WHERE you want to be, then you need to go through Chapter 1 again.
>
> It is important that you know your destination first before you set off on your journey.

If your destination is a long way from where you currently are, all you need to do for now is to identify your 3) <u>next accessible stop</u> (STOP A).

Your *next accessible stop (STOP A)* is the small action step that you CAN and MUST take to get the ball rolling.

> Your next accessible stop needs to be simple and doable – otherwise, fear could kick in and you may end up not doing it.
>
> It is important that you make Stop A as accessible as you can and get to it as soon as possible. **Do not delay.**
>
> Reaching STOP A will get you closer to your destination and will give you a better understanding of the next steps you will need to take.
>
> From there, you can identify your next accessible stop, and then the next one, and then the next one, and so on and so forth, until you get to where you want to be.

You DON'T need to identify all the stops and have it all planned out in one go.

> You just need to know where you currently are, where you ultimately want to be, and your next accessible stop.
>
> Take a step at a time and keep going until you reach your destination.

CAUTION: The road ahead may not be a straight and paved path.

Your path may zig-zag.

It may have pits and bumps.

Gosh, it may even have dead-ends and cliffs like mine, which is why you may also need to take U-turns and try another route sometimes.

It doesn't matter if you don't follow the original path you set out to take.

As long as you have your final destination in mind, then you should be able to get there in the end, regardless of which path you take.

Let's get some inspiration from the story of American filmmaker and creator of the Star Wars and Indiana Jones franchises, **George Lucas.** Sharing his life's experiences at the Academy of Achievement, he said,

> *"Everything I did I always followed something that I cared about. Something that I loved. Something I was passionate about.*
>
> *And I kept following that passion, whether it was cars, whether it was anthropology, whether it was art, photography... Eventually, it led me to my huge passion, my real passion, which was making movies, which combined all of those things.*
>
> *And I realized that had I gone to get my degree in anthropology, I would have probably made anthropological movies in New Guinea or someplace, and eventually been on National Geographic, and the History Channel, and then making features, and then I had done Star Wars just the same.*
>
> *If I'd gone into an arts center and become an illustrator, I would have probably started doing animation and doing animated films and making animated things and ultimately I would have gone on and been right where I was.*
>
> *So, no matter which route I took because I cared about all of them, they all led to the same place."*
>
> SOURCE: Academy of Achievement

So, follow your passion, take a step at a time, and you'll get to where you need to be eventually.

Uh, just one problem….
I don't know what my next accessible stop is.
I will be STUCK here forever!

Calm down, don't panic. Help is on the way.

You can ask for directions!

STEP 2: ASK FOR DIRECTIONS

There are several ways to ask for directions:

a. **Read**.

There is so much freely available information out there that you can draw inspiration from – books, blogs and many informational guides can help you get started.

Use your library. Surf the web.

To avoid feeling overwhelmed, focus only on one or two sources at a time, and reflect on what you need to do next.

b. **Sign up for a course.**

This may help you to get some structure and understanding of what you need to do.

Courses do not necessarily have to be University-level courses that take years and years to complete (unless your heart is set to do something that requires a degree, e.g., becoming a nurse).

There are community courses, or even short, online courses, that you can tap into to suit your learning needs. Look for a good one and ask for recommendations from people in the know.

There are also many free and flexible ways to learn new skills these days. There are plenty of free tutorials online that can trigger more curiosity and learning.

However, the risk of feeling overwhelmed is a possibility – there's too much information out there!

So be sure to focus on one good source (or two), and then reflect on what you need to do next.

For example, although I am an experienced academic with a proven track record of scientific publications, I knew publishing in academia wasn't going to be enough.

If I wanted to share what I know and really make a difference, I knew I had to move out of my comfort zone (i.e., engage with an audience outside my inner circle).

But how would I do that?

Sure, I knew how to write (admittedly, mostly articles that are full of jargon and scientific blah!).

But I didn't have the faintest idea of how to publish a book that can reach mass audiences.

- What should I do?
- What are the steps?
- Whom do I need to work with?
- Where do I even begin?

I was clueless!

Did that stop me?

Of course not.

Instead, I went on a course and learned from the best.

I knew I wasn't the first to go through this process. I just needed to learn from those who had been there and done that already!

In my case, I took a course from 9x best-selling author and Top 100 Business Author, Gundi Gabrielle, and learned a few ninja tricks about publishing from her.

Taking her course helped me to clarify the steps I needed to take to publish this book. She also showed me tools that can help me find my way around the market so my audience can also find my work, use it, and hopefully love it!

Gundi didn't just demystify the process for me. She also empowered me to say, *"Hey, I can do that too!"*

Knowing what to do is one thing. Having the confidence to apply what you know and actually do it is another.

The course also didn't take years, not even months, to complete. In fact, it only took me one whole weekend to finish it.

In the end, did the course work?

You tell me.

Without it, you probably wouldn't be reading this book right now!

c. **Talk to people.**

This is my favorite and probably most used strategy.

It's really simple – just ask people for direction!

Remember, you don't need to re-invent the wheel.

There may be others who are on a similar adventure or have already reached your destination before you.

Find role models and look for inspiration.

Learn from them. Share your journey with them.

	INNER CRITIC ALERT
	I don't know anyone to ask. Even if I do, I don't have what it takes to talk to them. I don't know what to ask.

That voice is getting in the way again, isn't it?

Let's see what we can do.

When your inner critic says, *"You don't know anyone you can talk to"*,

You answer, *"Really? Nobody? Not even one person?"*

Dig deep and think about who you can possibly talk to.

> Is there someone in your immediate circle who might have some insight into the life journey you would like to take?
>
> Perhaps a former teacher?
>
> How about your pastor or religious leader?
>
> What about a parent, a sibling or your partner?
>
> If they aren't suitable, perhaps your closest friends and allies can point you toward someone else who might know a thing or two that will be valuable to you.

This is the power of NETWORKING.

> You might not know someone who can help you – but someone you know might know someone who can.
>
> All you need to do is *ask*.

In my case, I re-connected with former supervisors, friends, and colleagues.

> They have given me their time and their knowledge about working in the field that I wanted to pursue.
>
> They also introduced me to other people who can offer more advice.

I also approached people online.

> The Internet can be a really powerful networking tool.
>
> Personally, I used LinkedIn and Facebook to approach people who can offer advice on how to fulfill my aspirations.
>
> There are also online blogs and forums that will allow you to connect with people who can offer knowledge and experience to help guide you in the right direction. For example, Parenting.com is a fantastic online forum that can provide support and information for parents.
>
> With social media, you can connect with people all over the world and learn from them. You can approach people who are already doing what you want to do.

- Ask them about their journey – what do you need to know?
- Where do you need to start?
- What advice can they give you based on their experience?

You'll be amazed by the wealth of knowledge out there and how generous people can be with sharing their time, skills and talents.

If you are worried that you don't know what to ask, well, STOP WORRYING – that doesn't help.

It can be intimidating and scary at first to approach people, but it's really quite easy and simple to do.

Here's what I normally do:

- Introduce myself (i.e., who I am, what I do or what I want to do)
- How I knew about them (i.e., we have a common connection or I found their profile online)
- Why I am approaching them (e.g., they have skills or experiences that I can learn from)
- What I need (i.e., I tell them exactly what I need from them. For example, I would say something like, "I would appreciate the opportunity to pick your brain and ask about your experience as a community leader.")
- Show gratitude (i.e., I thank them for reading my message)
- Anticipate a response (i.e., I would say that I look forward to hearing from them soon)
- Keep in contact (i.e., I leave my contact details so they can reply to my message if they wish)

INNER CRITIC ALERT
I am afraid they will make fun of me. They might just ignore me. I will look stupid.

I used to worry that people I approached would make fun of me or that they would just ignore me.

But believe me, from my experience, people have been surprisingly helpful when I ask nicely.

It is really refreshing to see how much people are willing to share, just so they can help someone else.

People can be truly generous.

I also used to worry that I would look stupid.

But somehow, I have brushed away that little critic now.

Asking for help is not stupidity – it's humility.

It's accepting that there are things that you don't know and that there are others who know more than you do.

Surely that's not stupid, is it?

STEP 3: GO!

You have your map. You asked for directions. You know your first stop.

Now, take your first step and go for it!

To quote Lao Tzu, *"The journey of a thousand miles begins with one step."*

Know your starting point, have the end in sight and take your first step.

Don't worry about the in-between. It will unravel naturally, especially when your purpose is deeply ingrained in you.

Don't worry about the *how* either – you will learn this as you go along.

Just make sure that you know *where* you want to be and *why*; which is why it is very important to have a statement of purpose and a clear vision of what you want for your life.

Take small baby steps, one at a time, and add more steps as you go along but *always remind yourself of your purpose*.

🏃	INNER CRITIC ALERT
	But someone told me to take the plunge, not just baby steps.

Whether you take a baby step or a massive plunge is entirely YOUR decision.

The important thing is you know your starting point, your destination, and your Stop A.

Stop A is YOUR next accessible stop.

Go for what is accessible to you.

However, bear in mind that what is accessible also depends on where you are right now and where you are heading.

For some, the next accessible stop only requires a small step because it is very close to where they are now.

For example, a journalist who wants to expand her reach by becoming an online blogger may only need a small step (i.e., change her medium from print to online) since what she does now is somewhat similar to what she wants to do next.

But for others, a plunge may be necessary because their next accessible stop is on the other side of the ocean!

For example, a Wall Street banker who wants to give up his current lifestyle for a quiet life in the countryside to pursue his passion for beekeeping will have to take a giant leap (i.e., quit his job) and ride the subsequent changes that go with it.

But remember, even if you are taking a massive plunge, you still need to also take a small baby step (i.e., make a decision to take that plunge).

For example, the banker who needs to quit his job to pursue his passion will still need to make that decision to pursue his passion and take a *small step* by writing a resignation letter.

He will also need to send it to his boss and negotiate an exit strategy.

But he needs to make a decision to write the letter in the first place.

It's that baby step that I'm talking about to get to Stop A.

You might also have an idea of what Stops A, B, and C are.

But to avoid feeling overwhelmed and become paralyzed by fear, you simply need to commit to reaching STOP A first.

How do you get to STOP A?

Take your COACH with you.

GO	**HAVE A GO!**

Get yourself to Stop A by taking your COACH with you

There are two definitions of a COACH.

This could be:

a carriage or vehicle that will get you to your destination; OR
a person who will support you to get you to where you need to be.

In this case, COACH stands for:

CO	Commitment
A	Accountability
CH	CHerish the moment

COMMITMENT. Decide and make a commitment to take a step toward your goal.

1. Identify Stop A: keep it simple and doable
2. Write it down

> There are many highly-driven people I know who write down their STOP A and *focus* only on this until they get there.
>
> Post-it notes are particularly helpful – just a little tiny note at a time to keep you focused and avoid feeling overwhelmed.
>
> Place it somewhere you can easily see as a reminder of what you are trying to accomplish in the next few days or weeks.

3. Make a *conscious decision and commitment* to take this first step by declaring it and saying it out loud.

> Don't be shy. Say it out loud!

ACCOUNTABILITY. Make yourself accountable to take that step.

4. State *exactly when* you will take this step

> Set an exact *date and time* when you will take this step.
>
> Schedule it.
>
> Add it to your calendar.

5. Hold yourself accountable by telling someone that you will do *what* you said you will do <u>and</u> *when* you said you will do it.

> Get them to write it in their calendar too.
>
> Ask them to *contact you to check* whether you have completed your task or not.

CHERISH THE MOMENT. Celebrate when you reach Stop A.

6. Share the joy of taking this step and celebrate when you reach Stop A.

***

So remember, take your COACH with you to get to Stop A.

If you don't have a go, then you are going nowhere. You are simply staying where you are.

Is that really where you want to be?

Take action.

> *Without it, all you will have is wishful thinking.*

INNER CRITIC ALERT
Hang on!   I don't understand why she's so skeptical about SMART goals when she's basically asking us to do the same thing!

Sure, there are similarities between taking your COACH with you and making your SMART goals, in the sense that these processes require you to identify a step that is specific, measurable, action-oriented, realistic, and time-bound.

However, the difference is that while SMART goals ask you to have it all figured out at the start, what this COACH is asking you to do is to just identify that one tiny step that will get you to Stop A.

As long as you know where you are and where you are heading, you only need to take one tiny step at a time to get there.

> You don't need to have it all planned and figured out, unlike what most SMART goal enthusiasts will ask you to do.

It's having the *commitment, accountability*, and ability to *cherish these moments* that will encourage you to take these steps, and keep going.

This will make the crucial difference between merely planning and actually doing!

Taking your COACH with you is also the essence of PAME.

We can go, *together!*

As an African proverb goes,

> *"If you want to go fast, go alone.*
>
> *If you want to go far, go together."*

You can take your best friend, your partner, your son or daughter, your mentor, or just a caring stranger you met along the way.

The journey towards your life's purpose is best experienced when you take someone along with you for the ride.

So what are you waiting for?

PAME! (let's go together!)

There are many reasons why some people refuse to take their first step towards action.

They have many EXCUSES.

Some would say, *"I'll do it when I'm ready."*

Translation: NEVER.

Others would say, *"I'm waiting for the right time."*

Translation: NEVER.

These limiting beliefs are deeply rooted in their consciousness because these unhelpful messages have been swimming in their heads for the longest time.

We will tackle that sluggish, annoying burden, called PROCRASTINATION, along with its father named, FEAR in book two.

But for now, the next section is for the brave ones who are *ready* and *willing* to **face their fears** and take their baby steps towards action.

If that's you, then keep reading.

CHAPTER 3

MOMENTUM

You have taken your first step toward action.

Congratulations.

"Now what?" you ask.

How do you keep going after you have taken the first step?

Simple.

Take another one.

And another one.

And another one.

And another one…

This chapter is about how you keep going, from one step to the next.

It is all about momentum.

Are you ready to keep moving forward?

PAME (let's go together!)

***

When you take your first step toward STOP A, you can go in one of two directions: you may get to STOP A (hooray!), or you may end up entirely somewhere else (uh-oh!).

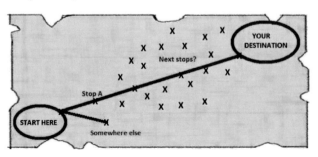

Wherever you end up, you will need to **re-orient yourself** before taking your next step.

Check your "map" and identify:

> 1) your destination (Is it still the same? Do you still want to go there?)
> 2) your starting point (new); and
> 3) your next accessible stop (new).

Your next step will depend on these bearings.

This is why it is important for you to review and reflect on these before your next move.

Let's examine these two paths, shall we?

Hooray, I got to Stop A

You took that bold step and eventually reached STOP A.

That's brilliant! Great stuff!

Celebrate and be grateful for what you have accomplished.

INNER CRITIC ALERT
My so-called achievements are too small.
They are not worth celebrating.

What you achieved may look small in your eyes, but this doesn't mean it's not worth celebrating.

Here are four reasons why celebrating your achievements, no matter how small, can be good for you:

1. It helps you keep track of your progress

> Celebrating your achievement, no matter how small, gives you a sense of momentum toward progress.

This helps you see that you are moving forward, rather than remaining stagnant.

2. It helps you to monitor what works well

Celebrating your achievement allows you to take note of what works well.

Once you know what works, you can try to repeat this process and replicate success in the future.

This repetition can eventually turn this process into a habit, thus making it easier and more efficient in the future.

3. It reinforces effective behaviors

By rewarding and celebrating your success, you are also reinforcing a habit to do it again.

My teacher's teacher, BF Skinner, taught us how behaviors can be shaped through rewards and punishments.

He proposed that behaviors that are reinforced tend to be strengthened; whereas those that do not tend to be weakened.

Celebrate your success to further strengthen your strengths.

4. It feels great!

Any accomplishment, no matter how small, triggers the reward centers of our brain.

Dopamine is released into our brain when we achieve something, while serotonin is released when we remember happy events.

These chemicals make us feel good and your brain will ask for more.

This will help motivate you to keep going.

Start a "catalog of wins"

When you accomplish something, write it down.

Start a journal:

- Note your achievement
- Reflect on what worked well
    - What contributed to this success?
    - Who helped you along the way?
    - Can you replicate this success in the future?
- Update your knowledge-awareness quadrant
    - What personal strengths came to the forefront?
    - Did you uncover new IDKs, hidden treasures or shed light into the abyss?

If keeping a journal is too tedious, a simple bullet-point list that you can update every time you accomplish something will be useful too.

Having this "catalog of wins" certainly makes self-promotion easier when the circumstance calls for it.

Preparing a resume for a job application, writing bids for an award, or simply updating a personal development review, will become a breeze when your achievements have been jotted down.

When in a job interview, you can pluck experiences from this catalog to highlight the strengths and achievements you accumulated over time.

This list can also come in handy when your inner critic starts yakking that you will never be good at anything.

When your inner critic starts the negativity, you can boldly flash this "catalog of wins" to its doubting face!

INNER CRITIC ALERT

I am completely lost.

I am absolutely clueless about what to do and where to go next.

When taking action, it is possible to end up in unfamiliar territory.

Don't panic. This is not uncommon.

However, if you were paying attention to the guidance from Chapter 2, then you should have learned some strategies by now to help you find your way again.

Remember, re-orient yourself and ask for directions if you are lost.

You may also try to explore alternative paths to take.

All you need is PRACTICE.

GO	HAVE A GO!

The PRACTICE model

Developed by coaching psychology pioneer, Professor Stephen Palmer, PRACTICE is a seven-step guide that involves:

Step 1	**P**	Problem identification
Step 2	**R**	Realistic goals
Step 3	**A**	Alternative solutions
Step 4	**C**	Consideration of consequences
Step 5	**T**	Target most feasible solution(s)
Step 6	**I**	Implementation of
	C	Chosen solution(s)
Step 7	**E**	Evaluation

The PRACTICE model is typically used within a coaching context. However, it can also be used as a sequence of guide questions for self-reflection.

Let's see how we can use this in practice.

Consider the hypothetical case of Sarah:

> Sarah is a student who needs to complete her thesis within two months. She is currently experiencing writer's block and feels completely lost trying to figure out what she needs to do to get back on track.

Here is how she used the PRACTICE model with her coach:

STEP 1: PROBLEM IDENTIFICATION

This step involves identifying what the problem is. You don't need to dwell on this step too much, however, it is important to note exactly what needs addressing before action can be taken.

Coach: What seems to be the problem?

Sarah: I have tried to motivate myself to finish my thesis but I always end up just sitting in front of my computer. I just stare at it for hours!

Coach: Is sitting in front of the computer the problem? Is there any other way to see this so something can change?

Sarah: Sitting in front of the computer is not the problem. The problem is not writing anything while I'm there.

STEP 2: REALISTIC GOALS

This step involves exploring what you want to achieve, in the *short term,* for your next stop.

Coach: So, the problem is not writing. What do you want to achieve?

Sarah: I want to submit my thesis on time.

Coach: What does that mean? What do you have to do to accomplish that?

Sarah: It means writing four chapters within the next two months.

STEP 3: ALTERNATIVE SOLUTIONS

This step involves exploring possible solutions to your problem.

At this stage, just brainstorm. Don't edit anything out.

Just let it flow – even ideas that seem outrageous and impossible are welcome at this stage.

> *Coach:* How can you achieve writing four chapters in two months?

> *Sarah:* I can wait until I get inspired to write.

> *Coach:* OK, let's write down *"waiting for the inspiration fairy"* as option 1. What else?

> *Sarah:* I suppose I can also write something, anything without thinking.

> *Coach:* OK, *"word dump"* can be option 2. What else?

> *Sarah:* Writing can be lonely sometimes, so I suppose I can also organize a writing group and block set times in the day to write together.

> *Coach:* OK, *"writing groupies"* is option 3. Keep going...

> *Sarah:* [continues to provide more solutions...]

STEP 4: CONSIDERATION OF CONSEQUENCES

This step involves examining the options listed from the previous step and considering their feasibility and potential outcomes.

> *Coach:* So, we have listed several ideas to approach your problem. Let's examine the consequences and likelihood of each option on a scale of 0=least likely to 10=most likely.

> *Sarah*: The truth is, I've been waiting for the "inspiration fairy" for months now, and yet, she still hasn't arrived. I really don't know if and when I will get inspired. I might miss my deadline if I keep waiting. I'll rate that option with a 2.

I'm concerned about doing a "word dump" because it might just produce gibberish. But I am getting a bit desperate. I suppose I can edit it later. What's the worst that could happen? At least I'll have something to start with. Hopefully, the "inspiration fairy" will pop in while I'm writing down anything that comes to mind. She has done that in the past. I'll rate that option with an 8.

"Writing groupies" could potentially work. I like writing in the company of others and I get my energy from being with other people. Being in a group will give me the support I need. But, I will need to find a writing group to join and that will take more time. I'll rate that option with a 6.

[continues exploring options and consequences...]

STEP 5: TARGETING MOST FEASIBLE SOLUTION(S)

This step involves weighing the consequences from step four and targeting the most feasible options.

Sarah chose "word dump" and "writing groupies" as her most feasible options.

Then she made a *commitment* to put these options into action:

Sarah set a date and time in her diary when she would start her first "word dump" and when she would contact a local writing group to join.

She also asked her coach to write these same dates in her diary so that her coach can check to be sure she does what she promised to do.

STEP 6: IMPLEMENTATION OF CHOSEN SOLUTION

This step is simply about taking action.

As promised, Sarah started her "word dump" and wrote parts of her thesis without overthinking. It was gibberish at first, as she expected. But, as hoped, the "inspiration fairy" did appear as she got into the flow of her writing. She also managed to edit her work when she had enough material to work with.

When her coach called her to check her progress, Sarah was delighted to report that she had written a fair amount for her thesis. However, she completely forgot to join a writing group!

After the prompt from her coach, Sarah contacted a local writing group and attended the group writing sessions every Friday at 3 pm in the coffee shop.

STEP 7: EVALUATION

This step involves reflecting on the process and outcomes of the experience.

It's about reflecting on what worked well, what didn't, what was learned and the next steps to follow.

Sarah managed to submit her thesis on time.

Taking the "word dump" worked very well and helped Sarah to release the initially reluctant "inspiration fairy". Simply waiting for her to pop in on her own didn't work.

Taking her coach with her in this journey worked well for her too and the prompt to join a writing group helped her to maintain her momentum.

She shared the joy of completing her thesis on time by taking her coach and writing group buddies for a "celebration picnic" in the park.

Sarah recorded this experience in her journal to remind herself in the future that this process worked well in this context.

Following completion of her thesis, Sarah's next step is to go on a speaking tour to share what she learned from her research.

***

Have a go with the PRACTICE model if you feel you are lost and can't find your way toward your destination.

Explore different options.

One of those options could potentially put you back on track.

Listen, you may have obstacles in your path.

But you are not the only one who has "roadblocks" in life.

Consider the following cases:

- This "rags to riches" story stems from a very rough childhood and steely determination to overcome defeat. His family was so poor, this athlete had to drop out of school at age 12. By the time he was 14, he stowed away on a boat to the country's capital city where he had to sleep rough for a while to pursue his ambitions. Although he didn't initially have any money to formally train for his profession, he took his sport very seriously and went all the way to the top. Today, *Senator Manny Pacquiao* is hailed among the greatest boxing legends of our time.

- This cartoonist experienced a lot of rejection before achieving success in his career. His work was rejected by his high school yearbook staff and he was also turned down for a position at Walt Disney. But he carried on with pursuing his passion. Today, *Charles Schulz* is well-known for bringing Charlie Brown and the much-loved characters of the Peanuts comic strip to life.

- These brothers had to endure tremendous difficulties before accomplishing their goal. They had to care for their mother who was terminally ill and one of the brothers had to drop out of high school to start a business. It took several failed prototypes, but eventually the *Wright Brothers, Orville and Wilbur*, successfully invented the world's first fixed-wing airplane.

- This best-selling author battled through depression. Before achieving success, she was living on government welfare and was so poor that

61

heating her freezing apartment was considered a luxury. Although her manuscript was rejected numerous times, the first billionaire author had to overcome these obstacles so she could give her child a decent future. For *J K Rowling*, failure is simply part of life. In her own words,

> *"It is impossible to live without failing at something unless you live so cautiously that you might as well not have lived at all – in which case, you fail by default."*

We can draw inspiration from the fact that we will all face challenges in life, one way or another.

Reflect on where you can draw the strength to overcome the obstacles that will no doubt stand in your way.

Maximize what you already have.

Dig your hidden treasures.

Seek help from others, if you need it.

It is very easy to look at other people's success without realizing that it took tremendous perseverance and support to get to where they are.

The obvious triumphs are celebrated.

And yet, overcoming failure and rejection, even surviving it and coming out stronger on the other side, is rarely celebrated.

Study failure.

Learn from your failure and the failure of others.

We have the freedom to keep learning.

When it comes to failure, my academic voice would say,

> *"If at first you don't succeed, try again two more times to gain reasonable confidence that it is not just a statistical anomaly."*

But what I am really trying to say is:

If at first attempt you don't succeed, try again.

If at second attempt you don't succeed, try again.

If at third attempt you still don't succeed, rejoice – you found a way that DOES NOT work effectively.

But don't give up.

Try a different approach to tackle what's blocking your way.

Perhaps your original approach was just missing something.

Figure out what it is.

Then repeat the process and see if it works.

MAJOR INNER CRITIC ALERT
Look what you've done! I am worse off than when I started. I shouldn't have gone in the first place. There's no way I could bounce back from this.

I'm sorry to say it, but yes, it is true.

You may attempt to take a step forward, only to find yourself three steps back.

But, this does NOT mean the step was not worth taking.

If you ask me, I believe that everything that happens in our life is a preparation of what's to come in the future.

Therefore, our life experiences – including the unpleasant ones – happen for a reason.

What this reason is will unravel in time.

Your inner critic might say,

"Easy for her to say. She doesn't know what she's talking about."

Please do me a favour and simply imagine this:

You pour your efforts into something you are passionate about. You invest six years of your time and energy into delivering the best that you possibly can. *You gain recognition for this.* You make plans to cultivate it and make it grow further, only to be stabbed in the back and be robbed of its fruits. While still on your knees, bewildered by what just happened, more sh*t gets dumped on you by the very same people who attacked you. This finally thrusts you, and what is left of your dignity, completely to the ground. To add more insult to injury, they throw leftover crumbs as consolation for your efforts. You are then left in agonizing pain, while those responsible walk away without the faintest idea of the consequences of their actions.

Your inner critics think I don't know?

Ha, they have no idea!

Just before writing this book, I experienced extremely challenging circumstances which led me to have a nervous breakdown.

Due to the sensitive nature of this experience, and the risk of damaging other people's reputations, I am not at liberty to disclose specific details of the events that led to this breakdown.

However, what I can share are the thoughts that came to my mind and what those thoughts meant to me.

See if any of these resonate with you:

What I thought	What it meant to me
I'm the victim.	I wonder if it happened because I'm a woman. Or perhaps because I just had a baby. Or maybe because I'm an immigrant. Or that the color of my skin is brown. Or maybe it was something else. Whatever it is, there's nothing I can do about it.
I will never get over this.	I am completely damaged by this experience without any chance of recovery. I am absolutely ruined. This is a dead end.
I'm a failure.	I gave my best and it still didn't pay off. I lost my self-worth. I lost everything.

What I thought	What it meant to me
Why me?	I have done nothing wrong to deserve this.
It shouldn't have happened.	This is so unfair and totally unacceptable. How could people behave like this?

According to psychologists Michael Neenan and Windy Dryden, these interfering thoughts are common blocks against developing *resilience*, or the ability to come back after a crisis or difficult life event.

> They have noted that resilience does not necessarily mean "*bouncing back*" from difficulties because this would imply that your life will return to the exact same state as before.

> On the contrary, difficult life events can change many aspects of our lives.

> > It can alter the way we see ourselves, our relationships and our priorities in life.

> > It can change us for the better.

> > But if we are not careful, it can also change us for the worse.

We are not the same person after extremely difficult life circumstances.

Neenan and Dryden also noted that just because someone demonstrated resilience in one context, doesn't mean they will be resilient in another.

> Each person has different breaking points in different circumstances.

> > Some adversities are more difficult to overcome than others.

> > Some wounds may take longer to heal.

> > Some may require more support than others, sometimes even from professionals.

In my case, it took nearly two years and numerous sessions with a mental health professional to begin the healing process.

The truth is, I could have stayed in the same position and wallowed in self-pity forever.

But my God certainly works in mysterious ways.

I was shaken beyond my wits, as if I was being told, "THAT'S ENOUGH!"

Let me tell you what happened:

It was nearly midnight.

All my loved ones were tucked soundly in bed.

I was in bed too, trying to get some sleep.

But I couldn't.

I was suffering from a pounding headache.

We actually just got back from Athens that night after spending the Christmas holidays with my in-laws.

It was lovely.

We had a wonderful time.

But as soon as we stepped into our house, I felt a sharp pain suddenly rush to my head.

I didn't make too much of it.

"Maybe I'm just tired from the trip," I thought.

Indeed, I was tired.

But it turned out, it was not just from the trip.

While in bed, still tossing and turning because of my headache, I started to think about the pile of student essays waiting to be marked on my desk.

"Geez, I have to tackle those tomorrow," I thought.

I never had a problem with marking student essays before.

But for some reason, the thought really bothered me. I started breaking out in a cold sweat and feeling palpitations just thinking about it.

And so, being the curious person that I am, I sat up to observe what was happening.

The palpitations started to get worse.

It was uncanny.

I tried to slow my heart rate down, but that's when I started to lose control of my breathing too.

I simply couldn't catch my breath.

I was hyperventilating.

That was when my husband woke up.

"What's wrong?" he asked.

I could hardly speak.

Grasping for air, I answered, *"I don't know."*

Then my hands started to feel numb.

The numbness started to crawl down both of my arms.

I got scared.

I remember uttering the words, *"I think I'm having a stroke."*

It was absolutely frightening.

Then I started to imagine what life would be like for me and for my family if I lost control of my physical and mental faculties.

I started crying and my husband ran to call emergency services.

Then my fingers started to clamp.

It looked as if my hands turned into crab claws.

They were so stiff.

My fingers were clamping my thumbs so hard that they both turned blue.

I thought, *"This is it. I have lost all control. It's time to let go."*

And I did.

I started to let go.

When emergency services arrived, I was back on track.

My breathing was back to normal, and so was my heart rate.

But more importantly, I was back on track to living a life with purpose.

That was my turning point.

It was at that point I decided to take a different path and re-prioritize my life.

***

It turned out it wasn't a stroke.

It wasn't a heart attack either.

It was a panic attack.

A severe one.

It was something that I have never experienced before.

As a psychologist, I knew about panic attacks.

Or, at least, I knew very basic facts about a panic attack.

But it was nothing like experiencing it myself.

***

After my panic attack, I reflected on the thoughts that had been interfering with my recovery.

I knew I needed to alter these, so that my mind, which used to work in my favor, could work for me again.

Here are the before and after results:

BEFORE	AFTER
I'm the victim.	It's not my fault but there is a problem that affects me and others like me. Some may deny it. But it does exist. It is structural and we need to tackle it.
I will never get over this.	Time will heal these wounds. It will leave a scar but the pain will pass.
I'm a failure.	This experience does not define my whole identity. I didn't lose everything. There are alternative ways.
Why me?	Why not me? I can handle this.
It shouldn't have happened.	Well, it did happen. But it is not about specific individuals. Heck, it's not even about specific organizations. It is about the structures and systems that people are in. Do something and work with those who can make the structural conditions better for everyone.

The events that led to my breakdown were necessary to help me re-prioritize my life.

Without sounding like a masochist, I am grateful that I experienced that kind of pain.

Otherwise, I probably wouldn't have written this book.

I might have just carried on writing academic papers, which only fellow academics would read.

That would have been the real tragedy.

***

In the end, does it all just boil down to personal strength and willpower?

No, absolutely not.

Some "gurus" may ask you to overcome your difficulties through sheer willpower.

They will say, *"It's all in the power of your mind."*

There is some truth to that.

However, there are problems that also require the support of other people's minds and actions, not just yours.

Considering the wider social context, when environmental conditions become so TOXIC that it cripples individuals from using the power of their minds, then it becomes necessary to call for mass support to effect structural change.

That will be the topic of another book, of course.

Watch this space.

CHAPTER 4

ENERGY

Taking the steps to fulfill your purpose in life is a fantastic way to spend your limited time here on earth.

It can be a truly uplifting experience.

However, there may also be a risk of burnout, if you don't pay attention to cues from your body and your mind.

It is important to have some strategies in place to prevent burnout.

It is also good to know a few techniques to "recharge your batteries" should you find yourself getting exhausted from your journey.

This chapter briefly presents 12 practical tips that you can use to keep your spirits up as you pursue your purpose in life.

These techniques are based on strategies from psychological research and some methods that I have used myself.

You may also want to download the *free bonus* that goes with this book to keep you inspired and motivated.

I have compiled **60 motivational quotes** from remarkable individuals from all over the world to keep you inspired and motivated.

Go to **www.thepamecode.com/bonus** for your FREE bonus material.

INNER CRITIC ALERT
These activities will not suit my personality and circumstances. It won't work for me!

Although these strategies may work well for some people, you may find that not all of these approaches are suitable for you.

That's absolutely fine!

Just pick whatever feels right for you.

Have a go at some.

Get a sense of how you feel about the experience and reflect on whether you can maintain these activities to stay energized.

I would also suggest that you try *one strategy at a time.*

Pick one and practice it faithfully for the next 10 consecutive days.

Pay attention to how it makes you feel.

Reflect on it.

If you like how it makes you feel, turn it into a habit and embed it into your routine.

Then, when you are ready, you can try another one and repeat the process.

Sound good?

Then let's get energized!

Are you ready?

PAME (let's go together!)

Tip 1: Look after your body

I'm sure you've already been told to eat well, move more, don't smoke, get some decent sleep, and so on and so forth.

We know all of these things already.

We hear these health messages all the time!

But for some reason, many of us struggle to maintain activities that are meant to be good for our body because of various personal and social reasons.

This is not uncommon.

When you decide to modify your behavior to take better care of your body, try to choose the easiest one to start.

GO	**HAVE A GO!**

Start a "healthy habit"

Try one "healthy habit" for a start.

> For example, if you don't have enough vegetables in your diet, consider making a commitment to eat an extra portion of vegetables today.
>
> And then commit to another extra portion of vegetables tomorrow.
>
> And then commit to maintaining your vegetable portions for the next 10 days, until it becomes a habit.
>
> Keep it simple and do-able until it becomes natural for you.
>
> When you've finished something you committed to, update your "catalog of wins".

Then when you're ready, you can try to develop the next "healthy habit".

You can start with simple ones and move on to more challenging ones when you are *ready* and *able*.

> For example, some people may find it challenging to quit smoking or to increase their physical activity.
>
> In this case, you may consider getting some support from your healthcare provider or from your peers.

There are also many proven techniques that can help you to achieve "health behavior" goals.

> If you don't know what these techniques are, ask for directions and take your COACH with you (see Chapter 2).

For example, if you want to lose weight and keep the weight off, you can consider learning about effective psychological techniques to help you develop essential skills to achieve this.

Health psychologist, Dr. Catherine Sykes has developed strategies that you can use for this purpose.

The same applies to other "health behavior" goals.

Also, don't be disheartened if it feels like hard work at first.

It may feel like an uphill struggle, but it will eventually become second nature as you embed these behaviors in your routine.

Research suggests that you need to keep doing something repeatedly before it becomes a habit. Take your time and enjoy this process.

Tip 2: Declutter your mind

Have you ever felt exhausted simply because there are too many things floating in your mind?

When this happens, take it as your mind's way of telling you to slow down. Take a step back and declutter your thoughts.

Meditation is a good way to declutter your mind.

GO   HAVE A GO!

Try meditation

The simplest way to meditate is to find a quiet and comfortable space that is free from distraction.

Sit comfortably, with your back straight (though not stiff), and keep your eyes closed.

Concentrate on your breathing and feel the rhythm of each breath.

About 25-30 minutes on this exercise would be ideal.

If half an hour seems too much at first, try 5 minutes a day to begin with.

Then as you get into the hang of it, increase more time as required.

Although meditation should not to be used as a *substitute* for treatment of clinical conditions, numerous trials suggest that meditation can help to alleviate anxiety, depression, and pain, and improve mental health-related quality of life.

If meditation does not come naturally to you, don't fret.

> There are many people who find it very difficult to "quiet" their mind and to sit still for some time.

Effective meditation needs a bit of practice.

> If you need help on how to meditate, you can consider taking a meditation class or you could look for meditation guides online.

Tip 3: Enrich your faith and spirituality

Enriching faith and spirituality has been associated with positive mental health and well-being.

In particular, faith and spirituality has been shown to help people cope during difficult times.

Reflecting on topics beyond what we would consider concrete and tangible could also help us to engage deeply with the meaning and purpose of life.

GO

HAVE A GO!

Engage in faith or spirituality-based activities

If you already belong to a church, mosque, or temple, you could consider engaging in more faith-based activities.

> You can attend faith study groups, religious retreats, community outreach, and other related activities to enrich your faith.

If you are not religious, you may consider reflecting on your spirituality or philosophy in life.

> You can pick a book, join a conversation group, or start a journal to record your reflections on your spiritual experience.

Tip 4: Reconnect with nature

Research has shown that we are spending too much time indoors.

Since the early 1990's, ecopsychologists have been generating evidence on how spending more time in the natural world can help promote positivity.

My good friend and colleague, Dr. John Hegarty, is among the pioneers of this movement.

>He has been practicing ecotherapy and other farm and garden-based initiatives to improve the physical and mental well-being of his clients.

GO

HAVE A GO!

Go out and explore nature

Find a place where you can get some fresh air at least 20 minutes during the day.

>For example, you can look for a place where you can see the sky, feel the wind, smell the ocean, and hear its waves.

If you are landlocked, try to find green spaces in your community so you can lose yourself in the midst of flowers, trees and fresh air.

If you don't have shared natural spaces in your community, why not make your own little paradise at home?

>Clear out your garden of weeds and plant some perennials, shrubs, or trees you can enjoy for many years to come.

>Make your own vegetable patch.

And if space is an issue at home, there are many ways to create green spaces in small spaces.

>Search online – you'll find a treasure trove there.

Tip 5: Express yourself

Being able to express yourself is a joyful and freeing experience.

People express themselves in many different ways.

> Some people express themselves through music.

> Others do it through art, crafts or literature.

> Some may also blog (or vlog!) as an outlet for their thoughts and emotions.

Whatever your outlet may be, it is energizing to have the freedom to express what you think and how you feel.

Find something that will allow you to express your thoughts and emotions.

> If you feel like singing, then go ahead and sing your heart out as if no one can hear you!

> If you feel like dancing, then go ahead and move your body like no one is watching!

Enjoy the pleasure of being able to express yourself freely.

> Just let your creative juices flow.

 HAVE A GO!

Have you tried chakra dancing?

If you are finding it difficult to sit still when you meditate, then chakra dancing could be an alternative for you.

> Chakra dancing is a technique that allows you to balance the energies in your body through music, movement, and dance.

To see what chakra dancing is like, visit ww.tinyurl.com/chakradancing

> Have a go to get a sense of what it feels like.

> You may find it quite liberating.

Tip 6: Learn a new skill

Learning helps with your growth.

> You can think of learning as an exercise.

> If you stop exercising, your body could lose some muscle tone and flexibility.

In the same way, learning is like exercise for your brain.

> You'll need to keep it active to keep it in tip-top shape.

Learning can also open up new opportunities.

> It can help you to uncover your hidden treasures and may give you new insights and creative ways of thinking.

GO — HAVE A GO!

Learn something new.

Exercise your brain by finding something new to learn.

> Perhaps learn to speak a new language?

> Or play a new musical instrument?

> Maybe you can learn to cook your grandmother's "secret ingredient recipe" for your next dinner party?

Whatever it is, try to find new skills that you and people around you can enjoy.

> When you've learned a new skill, remember to update your "catalog of wins" too.

Tip 7: Use your senses

As children, we have been taught that we have five basic senses: vision, smell, hearing, taste, and touch.

However, it has been argued that we have far more than just five senses.

Some would say we have at least 21 different senses.

This would include specific sensations such as pain, temperature, and balance, as well as internal sensations such as the feeling of butterflies in the stomach, blood pressure, sugar levels, a full bladder, and so on.

Others would go as far as saying we have more than a thousand senses, considering that just our nose has hundreds of scent receptors and can detect at least a trillion different smells.

Whether we have five senses or thousands, consider exploring your world with your senses and take delight in experiencing each sensation as it happens. You may find it rejuvenating.

I've learned the value of this from my mother-in-law.

Whenever we go out to have a stroll in the park, she doesn't just walk around and look at the flowers.

She literally stops to smell the roses and takes delight in this experience.

She takes the time to touch the leaves and feel its texture.

Sometimes, she even tells stories about previous experiences associated with these sensations.

Stories of her youth or the fun times she spent with her young children while being surrounded by trees and flowers.

She takes pleasure in the goodness around her as she reflects on the past, present, and future goodness these sensations bring to her.

Savor goodness with your senses

Enjoy the world with your senses.

When eating your food, don't just gobble it up.

Take delight in the different colors of your food.

Sense the different aromas, flavors and textures in your mouth. Hear the different sounds of your meal (e.g., the crackle of every bite; the pouring liquid of your drink).

Feel the temperature and sense how it makes your body feel.

Do the same when you go to sleep.

Appreciate the colors and scents of your room.

Sense the sounds, textures and comfort around you.

Feel the warmth of your bed and cherish it.

Sense how it makes your body feel.

Take time to appreciate these simple pleasures.

Tip 8: Be grateful (and express it!)

While we're on the subject of cherishing goodness, you may as well be grateful for all the goodness that you have in your life.

We already know how important it is to appreciate your successes (see Chapter 3).

The same goes for the goodness you experience in your life, no matter how big or small.

Being grateful for what you have can also prevent you from diving into what Mark Twain called "the death of joy", i.e., social comparison.

Rather than wishing that you have someone else's life, being grateful for what you have allows you to appreciate your life more.

It will also help you to focus on the positive things in your life and expand on these.

In addition, being grateful and *expressing it*, will help you share the joy in your life with others.

Express your appreciation to people who bring joy to your life.

Thank people in your innermost circle and those whom you've never thanked before.

Thank the bus driver for getting you to your destination.

Send your compliments to the chef for the glorious food on your dinner plate.

Express your gratitude to your religious leader for that inspirational sermon.

Express your gratitude with sincerity.

You can say it in person.

Or you can send a personal card, a letter, a voicemail, or a message on social media.

You may also include them in your thanksgiving prayers if you are religious.

GO

HAVE A GO!

Say "thank you" with a sincere smile.

Next time you say "thank you", try to pause and say it with a *sincere smile*. When you smile, use your lips, as well as your eyes.

Be aware and take some time to notice how the person received your thanks and your smile.

Taking a bit of time to say "thank you", with a sincere smile, can really brighten someone's day.

Tip 9: Practice random acts of kindness

Do you notice that when you help other people, you not only feel good about what you are doing, but you usually also feel good about yourself?

Whether it is simply offering someone a seat on the train, or offering to wash the dishes because your partner is tired, doing something good for someone else also can make us feel good too.

Research has shown that practicing random acts of kindness can influence positive mood.

GO

HAVE A GO!

Show kindness to others

Do something good for someone else. Here are some ideas:

Donate at your local food bank or volunteer if they need help.

Offer to babysit for a friend so they can take a bit of time to rest.

Visit someone who you think may be lonely. You may also offer to cook a warm meal for them, especially if they are struggling to do this themselves.

When you practice random acts of kindness, try to expand your kindness more widely too.

Show kindness, not just to people you know, but also to strangers, even if they never know that you helped them.

You may also show kindness toward all living things – not just humans.

Don't limit your kindness to your nearest and dearest.

Widen your circle of kindness and keep expanding this circle.

Tip 10: Enrich social bonds

My social bonds are very important to me.

Although I do enjoy the occasional "alone time", knowing that I have people around me who truly care for me gives me the confidence and reassurance I need in my life.

I also don't have a gazillion friends – I've never been the popular one.

But the few ones that I have, I know, are real and genuine.

Friends who, even if we don't see each other for months, sometimes even years, I know when I need them, or when they need me, we can always just pick up where we left off.

Social bonds are very important for our health and well-being.

Having a sense of belonging is a basic human need.

There is vast research evidence that suggests how having meaningful social relationships can improve health, strengthen immune functioning, and promote coping mechanisms during stressful situations.

Indeed, having a connection with others is vital for humans to thrive and flourish.

Appreciate and celebrate your social bonds

Pick someone you care about and find something to do to nurture or celebrate your relationship. Here are some ideas:

Call a childhood friend and invite them for a catch-up.

Cook a special meal for your partner.

Take a friend with you to visit a loved ones' grave and say a thanksgiving prayer for the time you spent with them (or if you are not religious, spend time to reflect on how your loved one's life impacted your own).

Tip 11: Give hugs

I love hugs!

OK, probably not all hugs.

I love sincere, warm hugs – especially from my son and my husband.

I love hugs from those two so much that my parents sometimes make fun of how much we hug each other.

We hug each other in our sleep and when we wake up in the morning.

We hug each other when we watch a movie together.

Sometimes we even hug each other as we go from the kitchen to the dining room, simply because we're all there.

I don't really mind that my parents find our behavior amusing.

For me, my husband is like a giant teddy bear – he's warm, cute, and totally cuddly!

My son is his miniature, travel-sized version.

And for them, even if I am this bony, little bitty of a person, they still find comfort and reassurance from the hugs they get from me.

It is not surprising that we feel this way about hugs.

Touch, especially hugs from the people we love, can boost oxytocin and serotonin levels, which can help to build trust and a sense of safety towards each other.

It can also strengthen the immune system and boost self-esteem, which is why receiving hugs can help to pick your mood up when you are feeling low about yourself.

It can also release tension from our bodies and strengthen the bond between those who are hugging.

 HAVE A GO!

Hug someone you love

This is really simple.

Just hug someone you love.
This could be another human being or your huggable pet.

And I'm not talking about a quick hug here.

Spend a bit of time hugging each other.
Cherish the hug and enjoy the company of your loved one.

Tip 12: Learn to forgive

Ahhh, forgiveness.

This is probably the one people struggle with the most.

I must admit.

I am one of them.

If we look it up in the dictionary, "to forgive" means to stop feeling angry, or resentful towards someone (or something) for an offense, flaw or mistake.

Sonja Lyubormirsky, the author of *The How of Happiness,* suggests that forgiveness does not necessarily mean reconciliation or the re-establishment of the relationship with the transgressor.

Neither is it equivalent to pardoning, condoning, making excuses, nor denial of harm.

Rather, it is about reducing your negative motivations and restoring positive motivations towards a transgressor.

This means, instead of feeling motivated to either hurt (e.g., revenge) or avoid (e.g., cut the relationship off) the transgressor, moving toward forgiveness is about burying the hatchet and moving forward.

In my case, although *vengeance* never crossed my mind, *avoidance* tends to be my default coping mechanism, which I must admit, is unsustainable.

But working toward *real forgiveness* is still something I struggle with.

How can you forgive someone when forgiveness wasn't asked for?

How can you do this when there is no regret or sense of wrong-doing from the other person?

Or is it really the case of forgiving myself, instead of the other person?

These are questions that I am still grappling with.

As I've mentioned earlier, just like you, my story is still a work in progress.

I am hoping to share my journey towards genuine forgiveness when I finally get there.

Take a forgiveness test

There are several "forgiveness tests" you can take online.

The one I would recommend is the Transgression-Related Interpersonal Motivations Inventory (TRIM-18).

When taking this test, think about your current thoughts and feelings regarding the person who hurt you.

This test will give an indication of your level of motivations for avoidance, revenge or benevolence.

Reflect on your score and think about how to work toward forgiveness.

For tips on forgiveness, visit www.theforgivenesstoolbox.com.

This website is hosted by my dear friend and colleague, Dr. Masi Noor.

FINAL WORDS

So there you have it! Change Your Life for Good with the PAME Code.

I hope this book helped you so you can live your true passion in life.

Just remember PAME:

P	Purpose
A	Action
M	Momentum
E	Energy

To uncover your *purpose*, remember PASTLE:

PA	Passion
ST	Strength
LE	Legacy

Be true to your *passion*, cultivate your *strengths*, and declare your *legacy*.

When you know your purpose, *write* it down, *visualize* your future perfect, and *embody* it.

Take *action*.

Forget about SMART goals.

Instead of planning SMART goals, simply START to act upon it.

When embarking on your life's journey, remember to:

1. *Bring your map*: set your starting point, final destination, and STOP A
2. *Ask for directions*: read, learn, and connect with other people
3. *And go:* do it and take your COACH with you for support

CO	Commitment
A	Accountability
CH	Cherish the moment

Stay *committed*, make yourself *accountable* to your decision, and *cherish the moment* you accomplish your task.

To maintain *momentum*:

- Celebrate your achievements, no matter how small.
- If you get stuck, remember PRACTICE:

P	Problem identification
R	Realistic goals
A	Alternative solutions
C	Consideration of consequences
T	Target most feasible solution(s)
I	Implementation of
C	Chosen solution(s)
E	Evaluation

- Learn from your experience if obstacles get in your way.

To maintain your *energy*, try to:

- Look after your body
- Declutter your mind
- Enrich your faith or spirituality
- Reconnect with nature
- Express yourself
- Learn new skills
- Use your senses
- Be grateful (and express it!)
- Practice random acts of kindness
- Enrich social bonds
- Give hugs
- Learn to forgive

***

I hope that you will find the lessons I shared in this book helpful.

Have a go at some of the strategies here, *reflect* on your journey, and *share* it with others.

For now, I wish you all the very best of luck!

Stay true to your purpose in life <3

E V Estacio 2017

***

Don't forget your free bonus!

These **60 motivational quotes** will help keep your spirits up so you can live your ultimate purpose in life.

Visit **www.thepamecode.com/bonus**
to download your free bonus.

***

ABOUT THE AUTHOR

Dr. E V Estacio is the Founder of the PAME Code for Purposeful Living (www.thepamecode.com) and My Life's Purpose Life and Leadership Coaching for Servant-Leaders (www.mylifespurpose.co.uk).

She is a chartered psychologist with over 18 years' experience in research, health promotion, and community development.

She sits on the editorial board of several psychology journals and is an avid supporter of organizations that promote literacy, human rights, and social justice. In particular, she has led and supported projects that aimed to promote the well-being of migrant and ethnic minority groups, children and young people, older adults, people with learning disabilities, caregivers and nurses, LGBT groups, and indigenous communities.

She is passionate about living a purposeful life and is keen to help others to do the same.

For more info, go to:
www.thepamecode.com

Or email:
info@thepamecode.com

PLEASE LEAVE A REVIEW

Enjoyed this book?

Then please leave a review on Amazon.

There are so many books out there. It will be very easy for my book to get lost in that ocean if readers do not engage with this book.

You can help others to find this book by leaving your review online.

Reviews are very important to give potential customers an idea of what this book is about and how it can help them.

PLUS, reviews will also help the book in its ranking system.

I would truly appreciate your support by leaving an honest review and recommending it to a friend.

Please go to your Amazon store online to leave your review TODAY.

RECEIVE A FREE COPY OF MY FUTURE BOOKS

Are you interested in receiving my future books for **free**?

"For free?" you ask.

Yes, you read it right – for FREE.

Interested?

Then apply to become a test reader of my future books.

As a test reader, you will receive:

- A free advance copy (ebook format) of my book.

All I ask in return is:

- A commitment from you to read the book within 1 week
- Give honest feedback on my draft
- Leave a review online when I launch

Great, huh?

If you would like to apply, please visit

www.thepamecode.com/launchteam

Made in the USA
Middletown, DE
05 January 2018